MADDOX

10 Must-Read Books on Starting a Fashion Business: Beginner's Guide

Contents

1

WELCOME

Hello everyone and welcome to a beginner's guide on starting a business in fashion! I am proud of you for taking this important first step; *the research*. You have this book right now because you feel drawn to the wonderful world of fashion. We are one in the same. The fashion bug bit me at a very young age and I could not think of anything else I wanted to do with my life other than something involving fashion. I took that passion to college where I studied Fashion Design and absolutely became enthralled by it all. With the amazement, also came reality. Maybe I did not know as much as I thought I did about the fashion world. I thought it would be just like the movies and magazines; glamorous and energetic. What I failed to remember is that when I visualized those shiny aspects of the industry, I was only seeing the finished products and end results. The runway shows, the big window displays at department stores, the high-profile magazines. There is a very long, ever-changing evolution from idea to execution that no one knows about unless you are "in the weeds". You do not just wake up one day and become a name or label that is recognizable and sought-after. How do you get to that point? How were these garments made? How were these looks curated? With so many different avenues, which best fits me and my skills? The questions almost become too much. Then, to top it off, the biggest question of them all.... **How can I turn this fiery passion into a successful business?**

I am here to bring clarity and share things that have helped find my place in the fashion industry. Could you search for these resources yourself? Yes, of course. But I have intentionally gathered all of the books together so you can skip running around trying to look for things to study and jump right into building your foundation. Coming from a fashion student and someone who is still working actively in the fashion industry, I want to share my favorite books. Some are more on the inspiration side and some are truly tools I wish I had learned in school. I was educated on all of the elements of design but not how to necessarily make a profitable business in the fashion industry. Or more importantly, help me figure out what avenue I wanted to go down and if I wanted to make it a true career or just a creative outlet/hobby. I decided I wanted to take my designs and create a brand. I wanted to be the one running this business but I had to teach myself first. I knew how to develop a brand but fell short on entrepreneurial knowledge.

Within this short book, you can expect a quick overview of each book recommendation as well as my personal stories. I have read each of these books and soaked up so much wisdom. Now I want to share! My hope is that everyone who reads this guide book will find it very helpful and full of inspiration. Please send it to a creative friend, give it as a gift for an aspiring fashionista, or keep it as a reference to utilize all throughout your personal journey.

2

101 Things I Learned ® in Fashion School - By Alfredo Cabrera with Matthew Federick

I have this sitting on my bookshelf right now and I am looking at it as I write this. Although it may be super tiny and cute, it is jammed pack with so much important information. Look at this book as your Fashion 101. I included this first because it really is the blueprint for everything else that is to come. If you did not go to any sort of fashion or design school, then you should really study this. It touches on every part of the common criteria taught in school:

- Identify target customer, set priorities, select fabrics, and other design details
- How to measure the human body (form), how to cut fabric, and other pattern skills
- The importance of understanding how a garment is made

- How historical events changed our understanding of fashion
- The fundamentals of fashion, body, and garment illustration
- Practical information on industry terminology, the fashion calendar, and more

If you did go to fashion school, you probably took a class or two regarding some of these sections. I can guarantee that you have forgotten a thing or two along the way so you can keep this book handy all throughout your fashion career. You may also be surprised by what new information you learn from the book! Regardless, this is an easy read and touchstone for setting the foundation.

3

Your Fashion [Dream] Plan: Turn your career dream into reality. An Empowering Actionable Plan to Break into the Fashion Industry - By Giada Graziano

You have decided that the fashion industry sparks something inside of you but you may be wondering about which career path is best for you. This book breaks down the actual potential within different avenues in the fashion industry. If you ever have doubts if you have what it takes or need help breaking through limiting beliefs, this is for you. Giada gets down to a deeper level under the passion. There is a sense of honesty as well as she breaks down the reality of what a fashion business is like; working for someone and working for yourself. The book covers:

- How to set specific goals, not just "something in fashion"
- Consistency and habit building in you fashion career

- Shifting your mindset
- Applying business tools
- Coaching and motivation

I would also like to mention that Giada offers a course to go along with the book for free. She goes through each section with videos and lessons as you follow along in your workbook. It is a challenge but very critical to better understanding your own personal goals and career possibilities!

4

The Fashion Business Manual: An Illustrated Guide to Building a Fashion Brand - By Fashionary

I f I had to choose my favorite book, this would be it. Somehow everything you need to know about being a fashion designer or building a fashion brand is wrapped up in this modern-day textbook. It is a step-by-step manual of all avenues of the fashion industry ranging from picking out fabrics to figuring out the floor plan of your future brick and mortar store. I received this as a birthday gift from someone *after* college. I was honestly surprised by much I learned. There were a few terms and just some general information about the industry that I had never been exposed to before. I found it very beneficial, even in my current career. Not only is everything concisely written, there are many helpful visuals. I am a visual learner by nature so even seeing some of the terms I had learned previously, animated or explained differently in this book was truly eye-opening. You can expect to learn about the following and more:

- Brand direction
- Product development
- Wholesale product
- Marketing
- Retailing
- Starting a brand or business

5

The Ultimate Boutique Handbook: How to Start a Retail Business - By Emily Benson

This is a tried and true, step-by-step guide for all of my people wanting to dive into retail. This is your opportunity to curate your idea of the perfect store. You get to choose every item to sell, how they are displayed, and overall how you want the store to feel. You actually do not need as much fashion knowledge necessarily for this path but it is very important to understand wholesale buying, business in general, and customer-driven mindset. This same handbook can apply to starting an online boutique. Today's society is so motivated to buy cute things they see on Instagram. I am included. Now, more than ever, the opportunity to get into retail is easier and more accessible- stores and digital. This guide will teach you:

- Target Market
- Boutique location
- Deciding what type of boutique is best for you
- Where to purchase products
- Budgets to get started
- Insurance and credit card processing
- Brand image
- Fixtures and displays
- Mobile boutiques
- Resources and websites

6

Stylist: The Interpreters of Fashion - By Style.com

Calling all aspiring stylists! Your bible is here. This is an iconic book foreword by Anna Wintour herself. If you do not know who that is then you are about to learn. Pro tip: do not be scared by the price. Feel free to purchase a used version for less! The value inside will never decrease. The fashion gatekeepers, designers, creatives, and more make up the sixteen powerhouses featured in this book. Ignite your love for all things creative curation. From styling for photo shoots to putting the last minute scarf on a model before she walks down the runway. You will fall in love with this book. Although it was published over ten years ago, the information still rings true today. Keep in mind, of course, that social media was not as influential back then as it is today so style trends are easier to pick up than ever before but this book is where that all started. Be inspired by breath-taking images throughout the whole book brought to you by:

- Annie Leibovitz - Photographer

- Cecil Beaton – Photographer
- Richard Avedon – Photographer
- And others

Learn from famous editors:

- How stylists propel the industry forward
- Intuition on what is next in fashion
- How photographers, editors, and stylists work together
- How to illustrate the taste of who you are styling

7

Freelancing in Fashion: A Step-By-step Guide to Creating Your Portfolio, Setting Rates and Finding Clients You Love - By Heidi Sew

Say you are great at a specific part of the fashion industry. It could be something like pattern making, illustration, personal shopping, window displays, etc. There is a way to make it your whole career. Doing the one thing you are amazing at and truly love doing. Other positions in the industry may require you to juggle a few different tasks whereas freelancing allows you the opportunity to provide one service to many different clients or businesses. I have personally read this book, actively listen to the podcast, and eat up any free downloadable resources this incredible author, Heidi, has. She has changed the lives of so many creatives who want to work for themselves doing what they do best. This is a guide on how to tap into your true potential to provide your best work while making sure you get paid your worth. You will walk through five steps:

- Figuring out what service or services you want to provide
- Building a portfolio of all of your past work
- Finding dream clients and successfully pitching to them
- Pricing your services what they are truly worth
- Creating a strategy for consistent work

I highly suggest getting into Heidi's Facebook group, signing up for her email list, and listening to her podcast. She is one of those people who is not a gatekeeper and will share all of the gems for anyone wanting to make a living off of their gifts and talents.

8

Business Boutique: A Woman's Guide for Making Money Doing What She Loves - By Christy Wright

The next three books are general business books and vital for success. When starting my fashion business, I had absolutely no idea where to start. I attended a conference where Christy spoke at. She pumped me so much to the point where there was nothing anyone could do to stop me from achieving my dreams of producing my own fashion brand, Nothing! Until I left and then the magic started to trickle away and reality crept in. I started to question myself and my abilities. Then I remembered she had a book that walked you through everything she spoke about and details you needed to know in order to set your passion up as a business. It is equal parts heart-warming and tough love. I used the outline of the business plan to really dig deep into who I wanted to be as a business owner. That ended up landing me a huge opportunity. Bigger and better than I could ever imagine. Because I was prepared! Here is what to expect:

- Create a business plan to start and grow your business
- Learn how to manage time
- Review pricing, taxes and budgeting
- Marketing to your target customer
- Selling yourself and products

9

How to Launch a Brand: Your Step-by-Step Guide to Crafting a Brand: From Positioning to Naming And Brand Identity - By Fabian Geyrhalter

Imagine you have this beautiful clothing line or chic boutique or have perfected a skill and wanted to offer it as a service. How will people find you? How will your target customer, who you hypothetically built everything for, find you? How do you want customers to feel when they see your logo? Every aspect of the customer experience has to be carefully curated. You will be walking through the importance of building your identity with this book. Take a look at all of the businesses on Instagram right now. There are thousands of boutiques, designers, freelancers, stylists, photographers, etc. Learn how to set yourself apart by look, feel, and sound to attract loyal customers. This is all done by intentional design. It may feel scary at first but this book will break everything down into tangible sections:

- Brand platform
- Brand name
- Brand identity
- Brand atmosphere

10

Starting a Business QuickStart Guide: The Simplified Beginner's Guide to Launching a Successful Small Business, Turning Your Vision into Reality - By Ken Colwell PhD MBA

If you are like how I was, you have no concept of how much a business start-up costs or anything about business for that matter. I did not come from a long line of successful entrepreneurs. Everyone in my family are extremely hard workers but have worked for other peoples' businesses their whole lives. I had to learn everything about entrepreneurship and business on my own. This is the side that is left out of fashion school and is why a part of me wishes I would have just gone to business school. Although this is not a book about fashion, it definitely applies to a fashion business of any kind. It will help you decipher your true intentions. Do you want this as a business or hobby? This book is the most important tool in order to properly start, maintain, and scale a business. You will learn:

- The difference between an idea and an opportunity
- Why being an entrepreneur is great
- The first steps of starting a venture
- Pricing, target customer, marketing, distribution
- Entrepreneurial mindset
- Finding your value
- Business plan importance

11

Big Magic: Creative Living Beyond Fear - By Elizabeth Gilbert

In any avenue you choose to enter in the fashion industry, there is a certain amount of creativity you have to tap into. Elizabeth changed the way I viewed my creativity with this book. It really is magic. Ideas come and go. You are basically digging inside of yourself and expressing your emotions through clothing, art, pictures, writing, etc. Us creatives really amaze me. We can make something beautiful out of essentially nothing. I am grateful for this book in several ways. Elizabeth has been a light in my personal life for a long time and now she has the most beautiful guide to help us find the "strange jewels" living inside all of us. This book is not about fashion, it is purely for the soul and imagination. You will receive new outlooks on:

- Attitudes, approaches, and habits
- Wonder and joy
- Creative process and unique perspectives
- Art and love

12

CLOSING

I wrote this with love. Love for the bright-eyed fifteen-year-old me who realized in high school she wanted to get into fashion but did not think it was possible. Who let others talk her into thinking about other career paths because of their mindset on how money and success were cultivated. I am so happy she chose to ultimately not listen and stay true to herself. That led me to living in a new city and sitting beside other like-minded creatives studying for my dream career in fashion.Then onto excelling in the entrepreneurial side of the industry. I always had it in me. I just had to tap into it. Listen to myself. Learn all I could and never stop!

Thank you so much for purchasing this book. Like I said in the introduction, send this to a fashion lover in your life or keep it for yourself to use as a quick reference for all of the curve balls in this wonderful world of fashion. I do not plan on stopping here. My goal is to keep sharing tools, resources, inspiration, and anything else I learn along the way. Maybe you will see a memoir by me about my whole career in a few years. It has been a wild ride to say the least but I would not change it for anything in the world!

I have personally learned from all of these books and I truly hope you do too. Buy the hard copies or download the digital versions. Keep them in your line of sight. Read a few chapters of one of them when you are feeling discouraged. It is a marathon, not a sprint. There will be ebbs and flows, peaks and valleys. Just do not forget why you started. We can do this!

If you found any parts of this book helpful, please feel free to leave a positive review on Amazon. This may be my first book/guide but definitely not my last.

13

RESOURCES

101 Things I Learned in Fashion School by Alfredo Cabrera (2010-05-20). (2022). Grand Central Publishing.

Benson, E. A. (2017). *The Ultimate Boutique Handbook: How to Start a Retail Business*. Stylish and Successful.

F. (2018). *The Fashion Business Manual: An Illustrated Guide to Building a Fashion Brand (1st ed., Vol. 1)*. FASHIONARY.

Geyrhalter, F. (2016). *How to Launch a Brand (2nd Edition): Your Step-by-Step Guide to Crafting a Brand: From Positioning to Naming And Brand Identity (2nd ed.)*. Brandtro.

Gilbert, E. (2016). *Big Magic: Creative Living Beyond Fear (Reprint ed.)*. Penguin Publishing Group.

Graziano, G. (2020a). *Your Fashion Dream Plan Book*. Glamobserver.Com. Retrieved August 7, 2022, from https://glamobse

rver.com/your-fashion-dream-plan/

Graziano, G. (2020b). *Your Fashion [Dream] Plan: Turn your career dream into reality. An empowering actionable plan to break into the fashion industry*. GO Publishing.

Sew, H. (2022). *Freelancing in Fashion: A Step-By-step Guide to Creating Your Portfolio, Setting Rates and Finding Clients You Love*. Independently published.

Style.Com, Wintour, A., Mower, S., & Martinez, R. (2007). *Stylist: The Interpreters of Fashion* (First Printing ed.). Rizzoli.

Successful Fashion Designer. (2022). *Sew Heidi + The Successful Fashion Designer*. Courses & Free Tutorials on Adobe Illustrator, Tech Packs & Freelancing for Fashion Designers. https://successfulfashiondesigner.com/sew-heidi-the-succ essful-fashion-designer/

Sweeney, B. (2022). *Digital Marketing QuickStart Guide: The Simplified Beginner's Guide to Developing a Scalable Online Strategy, Finding Your Customers, and Profitably . . . Your Business* (*QuickStart Guides*^{TM} *- Business*). ClydeBank Media LLC.

Wright, C. (2017). *Business Boutique: A Woman's Guide for Making Money Doing What She Loves*. Ramsey Press.